D0572911

CRESCENT BOOKS

NEW YORK

# WORLD TRADE CENTER

## TRIBUTE AND REMEMBRANCE

CAROL M. HIGHSMITH

obody had ever built such a city within a city—a cluster of buildings, including two giants, rising and rising from a gigantic concrete-and-steel "bathtub" set in bedrock. To make room for it on the southern tip of Manhattan, the Port Authority of New York and New Jersey in the mid-1960s demolished two tired fifty-story buildings owned by a bankrupt railroad and a welter of "radio row" shops. Landfill was added, forever changing the landscape of Lower Manhattan. When completed in 1972 and 1973, the majestic 110-story towers, at 1,362 and 1,368 feet, were for a short time the world's loftiest new skyscrapers. They formed the center of the new community of Battery Park City, including hotels, restaurants, smaller office buildings, apartment houses, and parks—a powerful economic engine that would pour life into a somnolent downtown.

It was all a dream come true for David Rockefeller, who had dared to erect a resplendent Chase Manhattan Bank building in Lower Manhattan and then pressed the governor (his brother Nelson) and others to crown the Wall Street neighborhood with something magnificent. "Catalytic bigness" was called for, he said. He got it and then some in the World Trade Center.

Constructed at a cost of $1 billion over six years in what *Reader's Digest* called the largest building project since the Pyramids, the trade center was an engineering wonder. Its sheer volume staggered the imagination. Angus Kress Gillespie, an American Studies professor at Rutgers University and author of *Twin Towers: The Life of New York City's World Trade Center* (1999), asserted that the center's subterranean levels alone could have contained the entire Empire State Building. The towers' anodized aluminum skin, laid on an outline of structural steel columns set just eighteen to twenty-two inches apart, gave the buildings a windowless look. The lattice of perimeter columns and a revolutionary network of cagelike trusses supported the floors, so no additional columns intruded into the office space. Central cores enveloped an astonishing 239 local and express elevators that whizzed past each other like a vertical subway system. Express cars whisked riders to "sky lobbies" on the forty-fourth and seventy-eighth floors. Automatic washing machines cleaned six hundred thousand square feet of glass across forty-three thousand windows. Transmissions from ten television stations and all the major networks beamed from a 360-foot mast atop One World Trade Center.

The architect of the colossal complex, Seattle-born Minoru Yamasaki, wrote, "Beyond the compelling need to make this a monument to world peace, the World Trade Center should become a representation of man's belief in humanity, his need for individual dignity, [and] his beliefs in the cooperation of men."

Skeptical New Yorkers took slowly to the twin peaks. Architectural critics called them outsized, boxy, an imposition—aloof from the action in Midtown and disrespectful to the beloved Empire State Building (1931), the Art Deco masterpiece that for forty years had held sway as the world's tallest structure. Conservationists gasped at the thousands of offices glowing through the night (the new buildings had no light switches). Environmentalists decried the sewage outflow. Broadcasters complained that their signals from atop the Empire State Building were bouncing off the trade center, causing ghosts and kicking up static. Migrating birds crashed into the towers, unsettling animal lovers. Word even spread that the buildings were un-American because a quarter of their steel came from Japan.

But the World Trade Center's visitors, numbering one hundred thousand *daily,* loved it—

Cass Gilbert's ornate limestone-and-terra cotta 90 West Street Building (1907) offers an anachronistic contrast to the World Trade Center towers that dwarfed it and the modernist Marriott World Trade Hotel, which was severely damaged when the twin towers collapsed. Lower Manhattan office space equivalent in scope to downtown Los Angeles was destroyed or mutilated on September 11, 2001.

loved the whooshing ride to the observation deck, loved the view, loved the shops, loved to snap photos of the double reflection at sunset. "The towers became a way by which people told the time, according to which of their clean, vertical steel girders trapped the brilliant sunlight," wrote Ed Vulliamy of the *London Observer*. The cues: "a deep gold on the eastern edge during early morning, becoming paler towards midday, and deepening again towards dusk. At twilight, the towers shimmered; at night, they were like pearly towers." Diners adored the two Windows on the World restaurants that, the *New York Times* observed, "seemed suspended halfway between the earth and the moon." A cocktail lounge was immodestly named The Greatest Bar on Earth.

Even workaholics laboring in the two aeries reported moments of serenity far above the din of the street and often above the clouds. On crystalline days, one could see into Connecticut, past Long Island, and forty-five miles into New Jersey.

Fifty thousand people—about the same number as the number of residents of Casper, Wyoming—toiled inside the towers for 430 banks, securities firms, law offices, shippers, engineering groups, stockbrokerages, private clubs, insurance companies, and the like. The lower levels were crowded with delicatessens and news dealers, doughnut shops, flower stores, shoeshine stands, clothing boutiques, and coffeehouses. Each floor boasted an acre of rentable space. All told, the buildings were said to contain 10 percent of all the office space in Manhattan. Early in 2001 the developer Larry Silverstein obtained a ninety-nine-year lease to operate the towers and five smaller World Trade Center buildings, which together had reported $88.7 million in income the previous year. The cost of the lease—$3.2 billion—was the most money ever spent on a parcel in New York City.

In 1974 a Parisian acrobat crossed a tightrope strung between Buildings One and Two. It was "the most beautiful place in the world to walk," he declared. Three years later an amateur mountain climber scaled the south tower in three and a half hours. World chess matches, a Valentine's Day marriage marathon, and rooftop rock concerts were held in the buildings. A New York spinoff of the Monopoly board game placed the World Trade Center in Baltic Avenue's customary spot; curiously, at $60, it was the cheapest place on the board to land.

After terrorists detonated bombs in the World Trade Center's parking garage on a snowy February morning in 1993, killing six people and injuring more than one thousand others, New Yorkers took a fresh look at the twin towers and decided that they liked them after all. The site and its surroundings were sought after for concerts and exhibits. The World Trade Center and Battery Park City—with their shops, restaurants, and waterfront, complete with walkways and docks for luxury yachts—became a popular place to spend a weekend afternoon or evening. Already New York's visual signature in the eyes of the world, they became defiant symbols of a great city's resilience.

The towers were engineered to withstand the high winds of New York Harbor, but they were not prepared for an airborne assault. Soon after the icons fell in the barbaric attacks of September 11, 2001, an indomitable nation, too, vowed to remember and rebuild.

Just as the World Trade Center towers were a vivid emblem of America's economic might, Arturo DiModica's three-and-one-half-ton bronze *Charging Bull* (above) came to symbolize New York's Wall Street (opposite), a few blocks away. Manhattan began in this toe of the island, which was settled as Nieuw Amsterdam by Dutch colonists in 1625. The entire Financial District took an economic hit following the terrorist attack of September 11, 2001.

Thousands of cubic yards of bedrock and more than one million cubic yards of dirt and landfill containing the discards of earlier generations were excavated before construction of the World Trade Center began in 1966. When it did, two hundred thousand tons of structural steel coated in aluminum and forty-three thousand panes of glass were assembled along Lower Manhattan's narrow, crooked streets. Six years and more than $1 billion later, the job was done.

The concept for the
trade center's struc-
tural system was
borrowed from that
of the IBM Building
in Seattle. Load-
bearing steel
columns along the
façade supported the
floors. The central
core, containing a
remarkable system
of short- and long-
haul elevators, stood
independently. A
five-acre plaza gave
pedestrians a sense
of the buildings'
scale at ground
level, an impossible
perspective for
most New York sky-
scrapers. Much of
the towers' asbestos
fireproofing was
removed during the
retrofitting that
followed the 1993
terrorist bombing.

The view from the World Trade Center looking northward encompassed two other famous skyscrapers: the Empire State Building (1931) and the Chrysler Building (1930). The Depression-era Art Deco Empire State Building (above) reclaimed its title as New York's tallest structure at the tragic moment of Two World Trade Center's collapse. The beloved structure features a popular observation deck, a mast designed to dock dirigibles, and lobby panels depicting the eight wonders of the ancient world.

The planned twin towers loom impressively in the amazing exhibit
*Panorama of the City of New York* (above), held at the Queens Museum
of Art. The 9,335-square-foot model of all 320 square miles of New York
City includes more than 850,000 tiny structures. The panorama was one
of the most popular attractions of the 1964 World's Fair. Support cables
of the Brooklyn Bridge (1883), another modern engineering marvel
(opposite), crisscross a distant view of the World Trade Center.

Like the World Trade Center's debut a century later, the opening of the Brooklyn Bridge (1883) sparked a redevelopment of Lower Manhattan. The bridge, which joined the thriving, independent city of Brooklyn to New York, its fierce rival, was the world's longest suspension bridge, its stone towers taller than anything in New York except Trinity Church's steeple. "With this bridge, the continent is entirely spanned," wrote one author. The World Trade Center, similarly, connected world commerce as never before.

An aerial swing
around the twin
towers begins from
the east, above the
East River. In the
foreground, South
Street Seaport
Museum and a
"festival market-
place" developed by
James Rouse helped
to save at least a
vestige of low-scale
buildings amid what
the World Trade
Center helped
create: another array
of New York sky-
scraper canyons.
Across this narrow
tip of Manhattan,
the Hudson River is
a relatively few
stones' throws away.

The approach to the
Staten Island Ferry
docks at the foot of
State and Whitehall
Streets was one of
the few places apart
from the streets of
Manhattan where the
scale of the World
Trade Center was
hard to appreciate.
Its towers loomed as
no other structure on
earth could but not
here, where they are
partially obscured by
middling high-rises.
Nearby, Battery Park
offered an oasis of
green amid a glass,
steel, and concrete
jungle.

This view makes
two important state-
ments. It shows the
clear dominance
of the twin towers
vis-à-vis buildings
whose height would
make them land-
marks in most other
American cities.
And it illustrates the
clever offsetting of
the towers. Because
the buildings did
not stand side by
side, viewers could
almost always see
at least part of both
and enjoy a double
show when the sun
played off their
shining facades.

By 2001 the glass-and-granite towers of the World Financial Center (1989), which includes the headquarters of Dow Jones & Company, American Express, Merrill Lynch, and the New York Mercantile Exchange, had softened the starkness of the trade center towers. Private developers never gave a thought to challenging the towers' imposing height, in part because they could never hope to accumulate the acreage that the Port Authority had corralled through the power of eminent domain.

For visitors to Ellis Island, across the Hudson River, the twin towers, when seen through the old processing center's arched windows, were an inspirational sight. At Ellis Island, where the doorway to America opened for hundreds of thousands of immigrants, the multi-ethnic faces of America appear among the stars and stripes of an exhibit (see page 1). Americans of all races and citizens of many nations died in the terrorist onslaught on the World Trade Center.

This classic Hudson River view makes it poignantly clear why the loss of the twin towers leaves such a shocking void in the New York City skyline and psyche. For a quarter century, boaters, northbound Amtrak riders leaving Newark, and visitors to Jersey City's Liberty Park had marveled at the stunning World Trade Center towers. With them in sight, there was no mistaking New York for any other city.

With its proximity
to Wall Street, the
World Trade Center
was a magnet for
foreign, especially
Asian, companies.
Among the tenants
were three of Japan's
largest banks, a
Taiwanese invest-
ment firm, a Beijing-
based oil company,
and a Thai chancery.
The Columbus,
Ohio, *Dispatch*
reported that
Bangladesh, which
had no companies
but dozens of
restaurant workers
in the buildings,
suffered the biggest
loss of life among
Asian countries in
the cataclysmic
terrorist attack of
2001.

The World Trade Center towers were icons of economic power. They were rarely called beautiful, except sometimes at dawn or dusk, when they attracted colorful reflections or twinkled cheerfully. Strength, certainly, as well as enterprise and ambition will be their legacy.

*This book is dedicated to the memory of those who perished in the World Trade Center tragedy of September 11, 2001.*

————

Photographs copyright © 2001 by Carol M. Highsmith Photography, Inc.
Text copyright © 2001 by Random House Value Publishing, Inc.
All rights reserved under International and Pan-American Copyright Conventions.

No part of this book may be reproduced or transmitted in any form or by any means electronic or mechanical including photocopying, recording, or by any information storage and retrieval system, without permission in writing from the publisher.

This 2001 edition is published by Crescent Books®, an imprint of Random House Value Publishing, Inc., 280 Park Avenue, New York, N.Y. 10017

Crescent Books® and design are registered trademarks of Random House Value Publishing, Inc.

Random House
New York • Toronto • London • Sydney • Auckland
http://www.randomhouse.com/

Printed and bound in the United States of America

ISBN 0-517-22092-X

Library of Congress Cataloging-in-Publication Data available upon request

8   7   6   5   4   3   2   1

————

All of the Net Profits from the publication of this book will be donated to The Children's Aid Society in New York. "Net Profits" are derived from the total revenues earned from the sales of all copies of this book less the costs of selling, manufacturing and distributing.

Since the events of September 11th, The Children's Aid Society has been providing emergency assistance for children and families in need, at its centers and schools and at other city locations where help is needed. Starting the day of the attack, Children's Aid mobilized its medical and mental health staffs to provide counseling, distribute medications, face masks, inhalers and other respiratory assistance; organized its caseworkers to help victims obtain assistance; and helped train teachers to identify post-traumatic stress disorder and cope with children who may be depressed or anxious.

The Children's Aid Society is committed to doing "whatever it takes" to help New Yorkers affected by the attacks, for as long as help is needed. As it has for almost 150 years, The Children's Aid Society seeks to help children lead healthy, happy lives and become productive, well-adjusted and healthy adults.

The publisher's contribution from the sales of this book will be used to help The Children's Aid Society continue to respond to the immediate and long-term needs of the children and their families affected by these events.

You can donate to The Children's Aid Society by calling 212-949-4936 or online at
www.childrensaidsociety.org
Or mail your check to: The Children's Aid Society
105 East 22nd Street, New York, N.Y. 10010

The publisher's contribution is not tax deductible to the purchaser of this book.

————

Text by Ted Landphair
Produced by Archetype Press, Inc., Washington, D.C.
Design by Robert L. Wiser, Archetype Press, Inc.

All photographs by Carol M. Highsmith except for the historic images on pages 6–9, which are courtesy of Tishman Realty & Construction Co., Inc., the construction manager to the Port Authority of New York and New Jersey for the World Trade Center complex.